80 10/15 .

00037751   P

for re

AN ENORMOUS YES
in memoriam Philip Larkin
(1922–1985)

edited by Harry Chambers

"On me your voice falls as they say love should,
Like an enormous yes."
(Philip Larkin: 'For Sidney Bechet', *The Whitsun Weddings*, Faber
and Faber 1964.)

"New voice saying new words at a new speed"
(Philip Larkin: Poem X in *XX Poems*, 1951.)

An Enormous Yes
IN MEMORIAM PHILIP LARKIN
(1922–1985)

edited by Harry Chambers

First published in 1986
by Peterloo Poets
2 Kelly Gardens . Calstock . Cornwall PL18 9SA
Printed in Great Britain by
Latimer Trend & Company Ltd Plymouth

ISBN 0 905291 85 9

ACKNOWLEDGEMENTS

'Dodging The Toad' was first published in *Poetry Matters 3* and is included in R.A. Maitre's collection *Blue Barometers* (Peterloo Poets, 1986).

' "This Is Your Subject Speaking" ' by Andrew Motion is a revised version of a poem that was first published in *The Times Literary Supplement*.

'The English Wisdom Of A Master Poet' by Peter Levi was first published in *The Sunday Telegraph*.

'Closing Lines On A Life' by Craig Raine was first published in *The Guardian*.

'Not The Place's Fault' by Philip Larkin was first published in *Umbrella*.

'Fiction And The Reading Public' by Philip Larkin was first published in *Essays in Criticism*.

'Point of No Return' by Philip Larkin was first published in *The Observer*.

'I Remember, I Remember' by Philip Larkin is taken from his collection *The Less Deceived* (The Marvell Press, 1955).

'Aubade' by Philip Larkin was first published in *The Times Literary Supplement*, December 1977.

Philip Larkin's piece on *The Whitsun Weddings* first appeared in *Poetry Book Society Bulletin* No. 40, February 1964.

Grateful acknowledgement is made to Faber and Faber Limited for permission to use the epigraph from 'For Sidney Bechet' from *The Whitsun Weddings* by Philip Larkin and for permission to reprint the uncollected poem 'Aubade'. 'As bad as a mile' is reprinted by permission of Faber and Faber Ltd from *The Whitsun Weddings* by Philip Larkin. Extracts from 'Here' from *The Whitsun Weddings* by Philip Larkin and from 'The Explosion' and 'Sad Steps', both from *High Windows* by Philip Larkin, are also reprinted by permission of Faber and Faber Ltd.

Grateful acknowledgement is made to George Hartley and The Marvell Press for permission to reprint 'I Remember, I Remember'.

Grateful acknowledgement is made to The Estate of Philip Larkin for permission to use the cover photograph and the photograph on page 68. Grateful acknowledgement is made to The Estate of Philip Larkin for permission to reprint 'Not The Place's Fault', the epigraph from *XX Poems*, 1951, 'Fiction And The Reading Public', the extract from Philip Larkin's review 'Point Of No Return' and the various statements by Philip Larkin on his poetry that appear on pages 56–59 of this collection.

Especial thanks are due to Brian Dyson, Archivist at The University of Hull, for permission to print the two unpublished poems by Philip Larkin and the doodles, drawings and photographs that were part of the Exhibition, *Philip Larkin: his life and work*, held in the Brynmor Jones Library of the University of Hull, 2 June–12 July 1986. All this material is copyright The Brynmor Jones Library. Photographs by Alan Marshall, University of Hull Photographer.

Contents

Drawing of Philip Larkin, by Howard J. Morgan, 1979 (22 inches by 19 inches.) From the University of Hull Art Collection.

'THE ANAESTHETIC FROM WHICH NONE COME ROUND'

Anthony Thwaite

Now what you feared so long has got you too.
The blankness has descended where you lie
Deep in that building you already knew,
And nothing reaches you in vacancy.
Toads and hired boxes all pushed to one side,
Lugubrious jokes made serious at last
There in the loneliest, cruellest, final place,
Your turning over of the wasted past
Has stopped forever. And you meet full-face
The shot that's never missed or fallen wide.

IN MEMORIAM P.A.L. 2.12.85

Vernon Scannell

I heard the news at one o'clock,
Formal from the radio;
The room seemed sharply cold as though
The air itself had suffered shock.

I was surprised by how those words,
So calmly voiced, could penetrate
The idling heart and resonate
Like softly falling minor thirds.

We met each other once, that's all,
Nearly twenty years ago.
We were not close and yet I know
His death-day stretched beneath a pall

Of melancholy that would leave
Something of its gloom behind,
A broken cord, half-lowered blind,
Although we may forget we grieve.

Of all that happened on that day
Of snivelling December rain
One thing chiefly chimes again:
I did not weep or curse or pray,

But petulantly cried aloud,
'I do not want him to be dead!'
He would have smiled to hear this said,
If he had heard from some high cloud.

Yet I believe that smile would be,
Although ironic, kindly too,
For who would approbate the true
Voice of feeling more than he?

PLACE-NAMES

"The place-names all hazed over
With flowering grasses . . ."
(Philip Larkin, 'MCMXIV')

David Sutton

They are worn and durable
  As silvered oak,
The old names: Coombe and Barton,
  Stow and Stoke,

Burying the land
  Leaf-litter deep,
Gorgeous as Arundel
  Or plain as Steep.

Improbable on signs
  The past remains:
A Norman lorded here,
  There died the Danes.

That dyke the Saxons dug,
  This river-name
Murmured its light sound
  When Caesar came.

Bless the namers, men
  Of pen or plough.
History, receive
  Another now.

Poet, labourer,
  They do not pass.
We scent them on the map
  Like new-mown grass.

LARKIN

Robert Hull

Like cloud shadow today
your death making its way

across England, across its towns,
counties, fields, lanes.

Slowly over cranes and spires,
and neglected waters,

along quiet branch-lines,
and college lawns

like cloud shadow it passes,
darkening recreation grounds,

estates with washing,
and slow widening

rivers. And you, going
ahead, at summer's pace cycling

down one of the lost lanes
at the end of the fens,

listening already
to oblivion whispering

from dusty stillnesses
where flowering grasses

hide the place-names.
In one of those faded Junes

you found somewhere
the start of a war—

queues of men, grinning
as if they were on the winning

team already,
the innocently

lived years ending
in spendthrift gesture.

Few such poems, all too few,
but no-one reproaches you

with this last silence,
though perhaps it means

you've let the literateurs
loose round the canals and choirs

to finally hunt you down.
But you'll be left decently alone

by the less well read
your compassion celebrated—

those being pushed to the side
of their own lives,

or adrift between garish wedding
and drab bed-sitter.

They'd be the best people
to come forward—

though they might never have heard
of you, it's they who could

best speak in your memory
their own felt testimony,

like an awkward 'Here endeth'
pronounced quite loudly enough.

STOPPING THE DIARY

Meg Peacocke

So, they have moved you to a harder bed
And changed the sheets and put the flowers away.
Somebody crisp tipped the Venetian blind
Abolishing the bleak December day
And stood aside to let the trolley through.
The same thick pillow props a different head.
Would you have been surprised, or would you mind
(As if you're there to mind!) hearing your name
Pronounced tonight to folk you never knew
In the respectful tone of public grief
Used for assured uncontroversial fame?
   Would it have made you laugh?

I wonder, sitting by a fire that blurts
And grumbles and grows reticent, where you are.
The muddied fields are empty, the long coats
Have stolen home for comfort, drink, a prayer;
While others, I suppose, disguising haste,
Eager to take a scalpel to your hurts
Are hurrying with credentials, files, notes,
To catalogue ironies and rhymes; confirm
Old-fashioned skill are in; declare what waste
It was, that puzzling unproductive blank
Of your late years; publish, and make a claim
   On quadrangle and bank.

That friendly gloomy face I can't recall
Except from photos; have no anecdote
About some chance encounter in the stacks,
No inside information; cannot quote
More than a phrase or two. The same hacked tranche
Of time is all we shared, not even Hull
Or cold northeastern valleys scabbed with brick.
Yet since you've snuffed it, how the dark creeps in.

You never took a stand, or tried to staunch
The draining out of hope, or begged a cure.
Odd how wry private truths of one who's gone
    Disturb and reassure.

DODGING THE TOAD

R.A. Maitre

I dodge the toad whenever I can,
being one of those men
who live on their wits:
pundits,

chatshow folk, touts,
gigolos, clerihewists.
It wouldn't suit me, being a clerk,
getting up in the wintry dark

to commute
in a *Hepworths* suit,
up and down those lines to the city,
five days a week to infinity . . .

each day the same,
tripping points through Clapham,
rubbing shoulders with brokers
and rubber-eyed bridge fours;

bum to bum,
in the Underground scrum,
with *Woman's Own* secretaries,
computerised actuaries.

Not for me, the swift half and pork pie,
the roving eye
clocking pantihose on bar stools,
stocking-tops under tables;

the executive case, its memos,
its bulge of *Playboys* . . .
Think of being them!
Ruled by the alarm,

the in-tray and telephone call,
the typist's unmentionables . . .
Think of being them, sad cameos
on yellow train-windows

when the lights come on at four
at the end of another year.
No, give me your arm, old toad;
I'd break it if I could!

VEILED QUESTIONS

R.A. Maitre

Up at 3, pissing . . .
Enveloped in mist, here could be anywhere—
Crew, Hull, Wapping . . .
No midnight sun of sodium glare,
garish on the skyline; or those
knowing winks from rooms' high windows.

Aerodyne rumble; a late
motorbike croaks in the dark;
sky a half-exposed plate
zincy with moonlight in that global park
of satellite junk, quasars' highways
studded with cat's-eyes,

warehouse of emptiness . . . void, now,
of that collage of pop-star lustre
and diamantine art when the Plough
and the Snake, Cancer, make you wonder
the end of pattern,
whether rosiness after a sodden

Winter's morning when mists lift off
like cataracts, sun-blindness
backtracks the years as you doff
a battered mental hat in reverence,
is no more than sun-glance off pylons,
if cleverest of almighty great cons.

PHILIP LARKIN (1922–1985)

Harry Chambers

Now that he's found (alas) his "silent room"
Beyond the sound of birdsong or Bechet,
Our ears are left those poems of more than gloom:
Enormous yeses time cannot betray.

LARKIN'S DEAD

William Scammell

A tall man, with thick specs.
No beauty much of face.
The alto voice erects
his doleful time and place:

England, late on, stuck
for policy, run out
of things to shout about,
money, time, and luck.

Back in the pavilion
he wasn't heard to say
'I could've made a million.'
He packed his bat away

neatly—he always did—
and walked off for his bus,
not himself, exactly,
and not exactly us.

We had a good time, once—
a woman, an idea.
Such transitory stunts
he thought small, bitter beer.

Which was his loss. Still
it flung him certain rights
to play the old Old Bill
on lost and lonely nights

collaring deception,
duffing up pretence,
charging all conception
with lethal lack of sense.

Here it was, loitering
with intent to intend
a queasy reconnoitring
of love, whose latter end

was clear in its first yodel
so therefore why begin?
Write *finis* on the cradle;
baptise the mannekin

with sundry cures for colics,
likewise a love of jazz
and hope his little frolic's
more gin than Vichyssoise . . .

And good luck to him. He
said true, sad, funny things.
Let Hull inter the body.
We've the imaginings.

Rare photograph of Larkin reading a poem aloud in public. Taken at the retirement presentation to Peter Sheldon, University of Hull Sub-Librarian, Service to Readers, 30 September 1982

"THIS IS YOUR SUBJECT SPEAKING"

Andrew Motion

On one of those evenings
which came out of nowhere,
and one drink led to another,
and then to another,

at well past midnight
(rain stinging the window;
the gas fire burbling)
you suddenly asked me:

If you could meet one poet
—they could be living or dead—
which one would you choose?
Partly to please you

I told you: Hardy. *Hardy!*
All he would say is: Motion?
One of the Essex Motions perhaps?
Then came your candid guffaw,

and just for the second or so
before I laughed too, I heard
the gramophone arm we'd forgotten
still slithering round

and round on a record, steadily
brushing the label and filling
the room with a heartbeat:
bump; bump; bump; bump; bump.

East of Hull, past the fishdocks,
the mile after mile of raw terraces,
the bulbous, rubbery-looking prison,

25

fields begin scrappily—the first few
spotted with derelict cars and sheds,
but settling gradually into a pattern:

a stunted hedge; a dead flat expanse
of plough or tussocky grass; another hedge;
another vast expanse; and nowhere

under the leisurely, washed-out clouds
a single thing to disturb the rhythm
until, like a polaroid slowly developing

there is the spire at Patrington—
a fretted tent-pole supporting
the whole enormous weight of the sky.

I told you about it, thinking
your church-going days long gone
and anyway never spent here,

but *Yes*, you said. *The Queen of Holderness*,
and closed your eyes—seeing yourself,
I suppose, as I see you now:

the new librarian fresh from Belfast,
pedalling off one summery Saturday
(sandwiches packed in your pockets,

grey raincoat tied on the pannier)
finding the church, standing transfixed
by knots of lushly-carved stone

in the nave's subterranean light,
hearing the tired clock, and feeling
that somehow no one had seen this before

or would do again, but nevertheless
convinced it would always be safe:
a shell as withdrawn as the mind,

where apart from the weary clock,
and wind rushing the leaded glass,
there was only the sound of your footsteps

clicking the wet green flagstones,
stopping, then clicking onwards again
as you finished your slow, irregular circle.

There was that lunchtime
you strode from the library
half grinning, half scowling
on to the Great White Way.

Would you believe it—
(your head craned down;
your office windows behind
bulging with long net curtains)—

I'm reading the new Barbara Pym,
and she says what a comfort
poetry is, when you're grieving
(but you were laughing):

"a poem by T. S. Eliot;
a passage by Thomas Hardy;
a line by Larkin" . . . a line . . .
And think what I did for her!

One particular night
you were prowling in front of my fireplace
half an eye on your drink, half on supper,

and in the mantelpiece litter of postcards,
ornaments, bowls of odourless pot-pourri,
discovered a jokey book-mark: "Some say

Life's the thing, but I prefer reading."
Jesus Christ what balls. You slewed
round on your heel to the table

almost before your anger took hold.
Later, carefully pushing your glass
through the elaborate debris of napkins

and plates shoved any old how
(so it seemed you were making a move
in chess, or planning a battle):

You see, there's nothing to write
which is better than life itself, no matter
how life might let you down, or pass you by,

and smiled—a sad, incredulous smile
which disallowed everything you or anyone
listening then might have wanted to add.

. . . but then again,
I'm really not surprised to be alone.
"My wife and I have asked a crowd of craps"
and "Keep them all off"

put paid to invitations, I can tell you.
Though there was the time
(you made a fierce deleting bleep)
wrote: "Philip; I've to be in Hull

from February second for a day or so;
I'll get to you at half past six".
What could I do? I had a spare room
but no furniture. So out I went

and spent a fortune on a bed,
a bed-side table, chest-of-drawers,
a looking-glass, "that" (you grinned)
"that vase." Anyway, he came and went,

and then a second letter: "My dear Philip;
wonderful to see you looking well. Thank you
for your hospitality, and jazz, and drink,
and talk." But not a word about the furniture.

Now look at this.
We were stooped side by side
to a glass display-case in the library.

Two poems in two days: "Forget What Did"
and then "High Windows". No corrections!
Well, not many . . .

Your writing ran
across the dark reflection of your face
in lolloping, excited lines. *Don't ask me*

why I stopped. I didn't stop. It stopped.
In the old days I'd go home at six
and write all evening on a board

across my knees. But now . . . I go home
and there's nothing there. I'm like a chicken
with no egg to lay. Your breath swarmed

in a sudden fog across the glass,
cleared, and showed you staring down
a second longer, reading through the lines

then straightening. *Not bad. But that's enough*
of that (one hand sternly guiding me away)
Come on. This is someone's subject speaking.

PS.
You know that new anthology?
The one that Mary Wilson edited—
the favourite poems of the famous?

29

Have you seen it?
Callaghan and Mrs T and I
all chose Gray's Elegy . . .
Why wasn't I Prime Minister?

The last place we met
(*If I'm lucky I'll know*
which is the last.

Unlucky, I mean)
was the Nursing Home:
buttery afternoon light,

a hot, boxed-in corridor
tiled with lime-green carpet,
the door to your room ajar

and you in your linen suit
watching the Test on telly.
In the silence after applause

or laconic reports, your voice
was the cold, flat voice
of someone describing someone

they hardly knew. *Nobody's said*
what's wrong
and I haven't asked. Don't you.

Well I've nothing to live for,
have I! Christ, don't answer.
You'll tell me I have. Like seeing

Becker at Wimbledon, winning.
He looked just like young Auden.
That was good. I'm sure I'll die

when I'm as old as my father.
Which gives me until Christmas.
I simply can't cheer up—

and don't you start.
And don't you go, please, either,
till after my exercise.

Like skaters terrified their ice
might crack, we shuffled
round the dazzling patch of lawn

and fed each other lines:
how warm it was; how fast
the daisies grew; how difficult

low branches on an apple tree
made reaching the four corners—
anything which might slow down

the easy journey
to your room, the corridor again,
and then the glass front door.

The trouble is, I've written
scenes like this so many times
there's nothing to surprise me.

But that doesn't help one bit.
It just appalls me. Now you go.
I won't come out. I'll watch you.

So you did: both hands lifted
palms out, fingers spread—
more like someone shocked

or fending something off
in passive desperation
than like someone waving—

but still clearly there,
and staring through the door
when I looked from my car,

waved back, pulled out,
then quickly vanished
down an avenue of sycamores

where glassy flecks of sunlight
skittered through the leaves, falling
blindingly along the empty street.

Two robed dons: Philip Larkin and Sir John Betjeman, after the latter's receipt of an honorary Doctor of Letters degree from the University of Hull, 7 July 1973

THE ENGLISH WISDOM OF A MASTER POET

Peter Levi

Philip Larkin, until his death on 2nd December 1985, was the funniest and most intelligent English writer of the day, and the greatest living poet in our language.

It is possible to feel about him, as people felt about Eliot, that he was the last great poet. His life was led privately and in the provinces, the job into which he drifted was obscure, and those who did not know him thought him a recluse. Yet no one was more loved, no poet I ever met was so entertaining, so generously witty, or such an enhancer of life to his friends, who formed rather a wide series of intersecting circles.

He was extremely English, as his poetry reveals. Ever since the Fifties, we have looked to him for a kind of acid wisdom at times when no other kind was acceptable. His most positive poems have an affirmative sweep which is unique; no one had the authority to imitate him.

When his shyness drove him to simulate an anonymous common man, he was most individually himself. His *Oxford Book of Modern Verse* was, as Robert Lowell put it, the ultimate Larkin poem.

When he was putting that together, he was very funny indeed about it, but also, of course, deadly serious. However gloomily he spoke about anything, his hidden or suppressed or unacknowledged high spirits constantly revealed themselves. It was as if at any moment he might break into a soft shoe shuffle.

His poems are full of ironies and double takes, and some readers have found them sour or severe or meagre. They are none of these things, least of all the last. I think we reject them only in seeking to reject ourselves. He found a place and a language for poetry when it had lost its place and language.

Of English poetry since 1945, his is the most memorable, and most of us know more of Larkin's poems by heart than we do of our own. He disliked public reading, and I have never heard him read his own poems, but the voice in them is so perfectly conveyed that one knows exactly how they should go. His friendship with John Betjeman ought not to have surprised anyone. When that remarkable man became Laureate, he wrote me a note saying "It should have been Philip."

Part of the strength of Philip Larkin was that he was a writer as deeply as he was a poet, so his poetry has prose virtues as the poetry of Yeats and Hardy and Eliot has. He wrote two most interesting novels, a volume of jazz criticism which appeared as articles from 1961 to 1971, many of them with obvious applications to the art of poetry, and the most exciting literary essays of my lifetime, collected as *Required Writing 1955–1982*.

His prose is both sober and brilliant, it is like wonderful conversation, it is completely unacademic. One could say of his poetry as he says of Andrew Marvell:

What still compels attention to Marvell's work is the ease with which he manages the fundamental paradox of verse—the conflict of natural word usage with metre and rhyme—and marries it either to hallucinatory images within his own unique convention or to sudden sincerities that are as convincing in our age as in his.

Both in prose and in verse his art conceals art almost too successfully. But one cannot think of a man as dull or his life as flat who dreamed up the sentence "Life seemed so flat you could see your own gravestone at the far end." The most memorable phrases of his poetry are even sharper, but it is curiously hard to quote them out of context, because whatever is said takes a whole poem to happen, a waterfall of ironies.

The first person in his poems is not necessarily identical with Philip Larkin. I am inclined to think that his simplest, most vulnerable verses may come closer to him than some of the comic and crusty attitudes which have made him famous.

He was profoundly decent, and he cared most about what we all care about. But he was also very shy, and the comedy was a sort of defence interlaced with truthfulness. His first collection, *The North Ship*, was a misfire, the second, *The Less Deceived*, was a classic.

Both his later books have the same energy and the same furiousness, but they show a widening range of tone. His achievement is 85 perfect poems down to 1974, not counting *The North*

34

Ship; no other English poet since Milton has ever written so consistently well. After 1974 he wrote very little.

Yet Larkin vivifies where Housman moons. Larkin and Hardy convince, where other poets fail to do so. Larkin and Eliot teach, where most poetry has nothing to teach. They are as individual as one could be. No new poet in English will be so well remembered for a long time to come.

(This obituary tribute first appeared in *The Sunday Telegraph*, 8th December 1985.)

With Anthony Hedges, composer of 'Bridge For The Living', of which Larkin was the librettist, 31 March 1981. The work was written in celebration of the opening of the Humber Bridge.

CLOSING LINES ON A LIFE

Craig Raine

Legend has it that once, at a dismally inept amateur boxing match in Hull, Philip Larkin turned to his neighbour with the words "Only connect." In its way, this is typical of Larkin. Not only that he should thus introduce a hallowed Forsterian nostrum into a coarse context, but also that he should yearn for aggression and directness.

Introducing Betjeman's work to American readers, he began with relish: "The quickest way to start a punch-up between two British literary critics is to ask them what they think about the poems of Sir John Betjeman." The nice thing about Larkin is that he was a reactionary. Or, put it another way, a counter-puncher. He enjoyed hitting back at received progressive opinion on Picasso, Pound, Charlie Parker and pulling out the troops.

His poetry, though we are used to it now, is full of explicit aggression against the idea of poetry itself. His first book, *The North Ship*, shows a young writer hypnotised by the example of Yeats, the old spell-binding tenor he was to repudiate with the help of Hardy: "When I came to Hardy it was with the sense of relief that I didn't have to try to jack myself up to a concept of poetry that lay outside my own life—this is perhaps what I felt Yeats was trying to make me do." After two novels, *Jill* and *A Girl In Winter*, Larkin returned to poetry with a voice of his own—a voice no longer straining for the top notes, but content with the middle range.

The note it strikes is apparent in the title, *The Less Deceived*, the authentic Larkin note of sceptical disenchantment. And a poem like 'I Remember, I Remember' takes the standard literary presentation of childhood, backs it into a corner and dishes out a tremendous pasting:

> Our garden, first: where I did not invent
> Blinding theologies of flowers and fruits,
> And wasn't spoken to by an old hat.
> And here we have that splendid family

36

> I never ran to when I got depressed,
> The boys all biceps and the girls all chest . . .

The negatives, the denials, are strung together like combination punches until the myth is counted out. "Deprivation," he once said, "is for me what daffodils were for Wordsworth."

Larkin had little time for poetic props and easy atmospherics. "Groping back to bed after a piss", one poem begins, identifying the speaker with l'homme moyen sensuel, before going on to ridicule artistic treatments of the moon as "Lozenge of love. Medallion of art". Larkin's chosen analogue for his art was the camera:

> But o, photography! as no art is,
> Faithful and disappointing! that records
> Dull days as dull, and hold-it smiles as frauds,
> And will not censor blemishes
> Like washing-lines, and Hall's-Distemper boards . . .

Larkin censored nothing on the grounds that it was unpoetic. His verse, like Betjeman's, was "resigned to swallowing anything". Even "Don't throw old blades into the WC"—a phrase taken from his review of *Summoned by Bells*.

A camera himself, rejoicing in disruptive accidents to compositional decorum, he once remarked to a photographer who was about to take his picture: "I tell this to all photographers: I am not bald. I do not have a double chin. And this doesn't exist."—"This" was his ample stomach. It wasn't vanity. It was a wry comment on vanity and its absurdity, followed by a rich guffaw. He included himself with the mass of humanity. And when Larkin praised writers it was always for this: his reservations about Tennyson ('vapid onomatopoeics') are balanced by praise for his "gruff ability to hit the nail on the head in matters of common concern". He likes Hardy because he is direct—a man speaking to men. He reveres Wilfred Owen: "His secret lies in the retort he had already written when W. B. Yeats made his fatuous condemnation 'passive suffering is not a theme poetry': 'Above all, I am not concerned with Poetry'."

Neither was Larkin. And yet, having disposed of it, having

written it off, having disarmed us, he can touch us easily and directly with the real thing, without the capital P. Poetry, when it comes, is earned, it has to live in a world where people grope back to bed after a piss, where people fuck each other up, where boys puke their hearts out behind the gents. Then, and only then, can the moon be seen for what it is:

> ... a reminder of the strength and pain
> Of being young; that it can't come again,
> But is for others undiminished somewhere.

A mixed blessing, is what one takes away from Larkin. But a blessing nevertheless. To return to E. M. Forster, his phrase applies in full to Philip Larkin: "Only connect the prose and the passion, and both will be exalted, and human love will be seen at its height."

In Larkin's poetry, the prose and the passion are not merely connected, they are inseparable, as they are for all of us.

(This tribute was first published in *The Guardian* in December 1985.)

TOUCHSTONES

David Selzer

In September 1963, Harry Chambers and I visited Larkin at his Pearson Park flat. Harry has already given an account (In *Larkin at Sixty*) of the visit (though *visit* is a euphemism where persons from Porlock are concerned!) and I do not intend to repeat the anecdote in its entirety. I do, however, want to add a detail or two to Harry's account and, in doing so, make a number of observations, mostly of an egocentric nature. Our attributing to works of art and to their makers the qualities we wish to find is a solipsistic, perhaps even sinister, version of the pathetic fallacy but, as readers, all of us are imperialists. At best, we colonise only a writer's work—at worst, make some claim on the life. I confess, in advance, to the former but hope to be innocent of the latter.

Larkin's hospitality impressed me then and humbles me now. I am, at the time of writing, roughly the same age as Larkin was when we gatecrashed. If I were, as he was, cooking the tea, getting ready to go out and writing to a deadline, my reaction to a ring of the bell by two strangers, whose motives *might* be respectful, would be somewhat brusque. Not only were we invited in (and ruefully, at that, rather than grudgingly) but I remember (how self-indulgent memory is at the best of times!) that Larkin commented kindly on one of my poems, a copy of which Harry had had the ultimate chuzpah to send him—either as a calling card or an advanced warning, presumably the former as the piece was dedicated to Harry. It was, more or less, about dancing and Larkin remarked that he was having trouble with a poem on a similar theme (the unfinished 'The dance', item 50 in *Philip Larkin: his life and work*). Mine sported a couple of lines of which I was particularly proud, their being, I thought, quintessentially Larkinesque: 'A dreamer/Due I'm told for no good end; a sceptic/Begging shrilly for someone's shoe toe' ('Excuses to the Empress' in *National Anthology of Student Poetry*). No wonder the poor bugger looked rueful!

An additional facet of the man's hospitality was our each receiving a couple or more of very large gin and tonics. The original bottle (Gordons, it was) ran dry and, before fetching a replacement, Larkin lobbed it (using the same action as that of a dart player) across the room and into a tall, wicker wastepaper basket. The bottle landed perfectly, cushioned by crumpled paper, and was followed, with equal success, by an empty Schweppes. Nothing was said—our host seemed pleased but not surprised. The lack of comment appeared to be in character (or, to be accurate in retrospect, at one with my perception of the persona of *The Less Deceived* and subsequent pieces) but the flamboyance, the risk-taking quality of the action did not. We had been privileged witnesses, as I realised in February 1964 when I read *The Whitsun Weddings* right through for the first time and reached page 32:

As Bad as a Mile

Watching the shied core
Striking the basket, skidding across the floor,
Shows less and less of luck, and more and more

Of failure spreading back up the arm
Earlier and earlier, the unraised hand calm,
The apple unbitten in the palm.

The poem, in all but one aspect which I shall mention below, is a fine exemplar of Larkin's talent—of both his craft and his perception. The pessimism, for instance, though it might appear on first reading to be at one with, say, Hardy's, is of a very different, humanistic order. The title itself, the ironic misquotation of an idiom, signals the stance. The lesson (and it is a piece, like so many of Larkin's, whose form, as well as content, expresses, however modestly and contingently, a moral) is that, in order to be undeceived, it is necessary to avoid the temptation—it is an *apple* after all—to be deceived. There is nothing *inevitable* about missing the basket with a 'shied core'—or an empty gin bottle—but when it happens with increasing frequency, it has more to do with the vicissitudes of age then with fate, and a considered acceptance, with 'the unraised hand calm' and 'The apple unbitten in the palm', is the only response.

   The poem's brevity, commonplace detail, demotic diction, elementary rhyme scheme and basically iambic rhythm belie the

40

subtlety of the rhetoric. The short first line runs on, after the briefest pause, into the second whose rhythm, syntax, assonance and end-stop *embody* the meaning. The third builds so simply, literally syllable by syllable, to the (in rhetorical terms) anti-climax, delayed by the stanza break, of the fourth and fifth lines. The caesura in the penultimate line prepares us for the final phrases, which, as I have tried to indicate in the preceding paragraph, amount to a declaration about the human condition, a declaration that, as a result of the tension between the negatives and the authorative movement of the verse, is both affirmative and sceptical—like 'Words at once true and kind,/Or not untrue and not unkind' or 'prove/Our almost-instinct almost true:/What will survive of us is love' (from 'Talking in Bed' and 'An Arundel Tomb' respectively).

The notion of a *touchstone* as a test for the presence of good poetry has always seemed to me a sound one. I am not using the term as Arnold does, where an actual line or two, from some acknowledged masterwork, may be used to measure empirically the 'high seriousness . . . (and) . . . grand style' of each new piece encountered (*Essays in Criticism*). My use is more platonic—it is the *idea* of memorability, the capacity for the lasting evocation of both the quotidian and (to use an appropriately Yeatsian word) the dream. 'As Bad as a Mile' stands the test well, memorable in phrase and in wit with the last line revealing, at its close, ranges of meaning—or what Seamus Heaney, writing about 'Sad Steps' (in his contribution to *Larkin at Sixty*), described as 'the symbolist hole in the middle'. What 'As Bad as a Mile', as an exemplar, does not have (and I am not implying that there is a fault in the poem qua poem) is the quality for which many readers acclaim Larkin—his ability to evoke not just the particularity of place and time but that of England itself.

After my first journey to Hull in 1963, I did not return until the late summer of 1985. My daughter had received her A level results and accepted a place at the university, so we went on a family outing across England on the M62. After Pontefract, the landscape began to evoke fragments from 'Here':

> Swerving east, from rich industrial shadows
> . . . swerving through fields
> Too thin and thistled to be called meadows
> . . . swerving to solitude

41

Of skies and scarecrows, haystacks, hares and pheasants,
And the widening river's slow presence,
The piled gold clouds, the shining gull-marked mud,

Gathers to the surprise of a large town . . .

and at dusk, on the return journey, crossing the plain (that encompasses Selby in the north and Doncaster in the south) of a century of pitheads, slagheaps and cooling towers, of post-war industrial dereliction and recent communal strife, lines from the last poem of the last collection:

> . . . and for a second
> Wives saw men of the explosion
>
> Larger than in life they managed—
> Gold as on a coin, or walking
> Somehow from the sun towards them,
>
> One showing the eggs unbroken.

A rare photograph of Larkin smoking, taken during the visit of Ted Hughes to the Brynmor Jones Library, 30 May 1975.

TWO UNPUBLISHED POEMS

Philip Larkin

1.

(an untitled poem celebrating the fiftieth anniversary—8th March 1979—of the opening of Hull University Library)

New eyes each year
Find old books here,
And new books, too,
Old eyes renew;
So youth and age
Like ink and page
In this house join,
Minting new coin.

(This unpublished poem, printed on the Brynmor Jones Library's own mechanical printing press, is item 51 in the Catalogue to *Philip Larkin: his life and work*, an Exhibition held in the Brynmor Jones Library of the University of Hull, 2 June–12 July, 1986.)

2.

By day, a lifted study-storehouse; night
 Converts it to a flattened cube of light.
Whichever's shown, the symbol is the same:
 Knowledge; a University; a name.

(Untitled poem written as an eightieth birthday tribute to Sir Brynmor Jones, October 1983. Item 56 in the Exhibition catalogue.)

SOME DOODLES

Philip Larkin

(Drawn on the back of the agenda paper during a meeting of the Board of the Faculty of Arts, University of Hull, 21 January 1981. Item 124 in the Exhibition catalogue.)

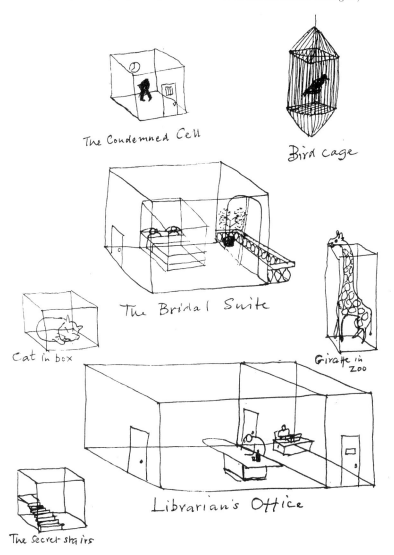

The Condemned Cell

Bird cage

The Bridal Suite

Cat in box

Giraffe in Zoo

Librarian's Office

The secret stairs

FICTION AND THE READING PUBLIC

Philip Larkin

Give me a thrill, says the reader,
Give me a kick;
I don't care how you succeed, or
What subject you pick.
Choose something you know all about
That'll sound like real life:
Your childhood, your Dad pegging out,
How you sleep with your wife.

But that's not sufficient, unless
You make me feel good—
Whatever you're 'trying to express'
Let it be understood
That 'somehow' God plaits up the threads,
Makes 'all for the best',
That we may lie quiet in our beds
And not be 'depressed'.

For I call the tune in this racket:
I pay your screw,
Write reviews and the bull on the jacket—
So stop looking blue
And start serving up your sensations
Before it's too late;
Just please me for two generations—
You'll be 'truly great'.

(First published in *Essays in Criticism*, January 1954.)

46

Self-portrait by Philip Larkin

NOT THE PLACE'S FAULT

Philip Larkin

In January 1954 I wrote a poem called 'I Remember, I Remember' (included in *The Less Deceived*, Marvell Press, 1956) after stopping unexpectedly in a train at Coventry, the town where I was born and lived for the first eighteen years of my life. The poem listed, rather satirically, a lot of things that hadn't happened during the time, and ended:

> 'You look as if you wished the place in Hell,'
> My friend said, 'judging from your face.' 'Oh, well,
> I suppose it's not the place's fault,' I said.
>
> 'Nothing, like something, happens anywhere.'

This poem was not of course meant to disparage Coventry, or to suggest that it was, or is, a dull place to live in, or that I now remember it with dislike or indifference, or even can't remember it at all. It is true that I could not today direct anyone to Binley or Hearsall Lane or Wyken or Stoke Park. But then I never could, even in my schooldays. And of course the inside of the railway station of one's home town is never very familiar, and I was certainly not likely to recognise mine. If I disregard journeys under supervision, a pawn in the hands of fate, I can remember taking only one journey by train—to Berkswell, to see John Greenwell—before I left for Oxford in 1940, and I really doubt if many others occurred. I am not a natural traveller: a place has to be pretty intolerable before it enters my head that somewhere else might be nicer. As I get older, for instance, I grow increasingly impatient of holidays: they seem a wholly feminine conception, based on an impotent dislike of everyday life and a romantic notion that it will all be better at Frinton or Venice; few men want a holiday, or work hard enough to need one. And I can discern this view in embryo in my reaction to the family annual holiday during the first ten years of my life. It seemed hard to be separated from my playmates and the series of complicated cricket games I was holding by means of cards and dice between the counties and the visiting touring team, and to be set down in a strange place without any of one's belongings. We usually went to Devon or Cornwall. I cannot remember details of any such excursion until the year when with what I now suspect to have been a kind of despairing malice my father arranged the family summer holiday at a holiday camp. This was long before the days of Butlin, but the essential characteristics were already in existence—the chalets, the communal meals, the forfeits and weekly initiation rites for 'new campers', the dances, beauty parades, baby-sitting and campfire sing-songs. Personally I enjoyed it—there was billiards all day, and no nonsense about walks—but it marked the break-up of our yearly holiday as a group. After that, we tended to go away in couples or with other people: my father in particular liked going abroad, at least to Teutonic and Scandinavian areas, and rarely agreed that more than one of us should accompany him. As far as I was concerned, holidays relapsed into tiresome interruptions of my precious summer freedom.

I should have recognised the outside of the station better, for I passed and repassed it daily on my way to and from school. Coming up the short, somehow rather unofficial road that joins Warwick Road by the Station Hotel took me past the line of station horses in their carts outside the Goods Office. When I went back at lunch-time they were wearing their nosebags, and on my return at a quarter to two there was a scatter of chaff on the ground where they had stood. I liked this corner best at summer teatime, when in addition to the man selling the 'Midland Daily Telegraph' there was frequently a white Eldorado box-tricycle that sold lime-green or strawberry-pink ices at a penny each. In those days newspaper placards bore properly-printed posters that today would look depressingly un-urgent. Beside the paperseller was a cigarette-machine, which gave ten cigarettes, for sixpence and twenty for a shilling (but with the twenty you got a halfpenny back under the cellophane): one of my fantasies was to unlock it and rifle the packets for cigarette cards. I sometimes think the slight scholarly stoop in my bearing today was acquired by looking for cigarette cards in Coventry gutters. There seemed to be a 'Famous Cricketers' series every summer then: Woolley, A. W. Carr, R. E. S. Wyatt (who went to my school), Kenneth Farnes, Freeman, Ames, Duckworth, Chapman, Hammond, all on green fields against cloudless blue skies; and then the Australians, the bland Woodfull in his blue Victorian cap, burly Ponsford, swarthy Wall, and Bradman, with his green Australian cap and crisp white shirt-collar, enclosed in a legend that grew bigger daily, like a gigantic indestructible crystal.

In childhood friends are necessary: you cannot bowl to yourself. I had none I remember until we moved to Manor Road; then I got to know Peter in St. Patrick's Road, and his cousin Arthur in Stoney Road. Arthur, a shadowy figure now, was a gentle, slightly older boy in whom I recognised for the first time the power to create and sustain private worlds. I can remember now his distress when our games did not tally with his imagined anticipation of them; the hours he spent playing rugger matches, enacting not only both teams but the referee and the crowd as well, with no other property than a clothes-peg; his construction of a complete chart of programmes for all the cinemas in the city, including mid-week changes, and his willingness to render any one we cared to pick. It was Arthur who with a kazoo and a battery of toffee tins, lids, pens and a hair-brush first introduced me to 'dance music', sitting buzzing and tapping his way through pre-selected programmes of current hits and standard hot numbers (how I now appreciate the artistic sensibility that drove him to render 'Ever so Goosey, Goosey, Goosey, Goosey' as lengthily as 'Temptation Rag'!). Once a friend left a tenor saxophone at Arthur's house, and together we reverently handled its heavy silver-plated intricacy and depressed the numerous cork-padded keys. What became of him I do not know. I think he was apprenticed to a butcher.

Later, Peter must also have introduced me to Tom and Jim, who lived further off in the Earlsdon area. We all went to the same school, and continued to meet for several years at Jim's house in Beechwood Avenue that had a tennis court and a sunk ornamental pond and two garages. Behind the tennis court was a line of poplars. I suppose it was not a really big house, but it was the first I had known where people could be completely out of earshot of each other indoors, and which had a spare room or two that could be given over to a Hornby lay-out or a miniature battlefield that need not be cleared up at the end of the day. I always supposed Jim's family to be richer than mine—at one time it must have been—but this was less because of Jim's many boxes of soldiers and Dinky Toys from Haddon's basement, and his frequent visits to the Astoria, than because of the airy hospitality informing his parents' house. The careless benevolence that produced Chelsea buns and Corona at eleven, and ignored the broken window and excoriated furniture seemed to me eloquent of a higher, richer way of living. The family were natural hosts. They had not to school themselves into accepting that a certain amount of noise and damage was inevitable if their son and his friends were to enjoy themselves: they took it as a matter of course. Looking back I can see that we were a great nuisance. I can only plead that we were very happy. One of my strongest memories of their house is of its long attic, that ran the length of the house, and which contained among many other things the debris of a hat-shop the family had once owned. There was a forest of hat-stands, small plush hemispheres on long metal stalks, like depetalled flowers, and cardboard boxes full of receipted invoices, wads of them, bearing dates of 1928, 1929 and 1930.

Before long Peter and Tom went to Tettenhall College, which threw Jim and myself more into each other's company. He was a year older than I, and left after taking Matric to become a master-builder's apprentice, but he had somehow got interested in painting. Together we took our education in hand: I lent him Lawrence, he retaliated with Cézanne. On Saturday afternoons we sat, frowning intently, in the glass cubicles at Hanson's, trying to decide whether both sides of the latest Parlophone Rhythm-Style Series or Vocalion Swing Series were sufficiently good to justify expenditure of the record's stiffish price of three shillings.

Our standards were very high in those days. The idea of paying nearly two pounds for an LP containing only three tracks of real interest would have appalled me. Jim's family took him away for their usual Bournemouth holiday, and we began to write—real letters, that is, not dependent on time or place: a correspondance to be continued, on and off, for the next ten years.

It now seems strange to me that all the time I lived in Coventry I never knew any girls, but it did not at the time. I had grown up to regard sexual recreation as a socially remote thing, like baccarat or clog dancing, and nothing happened to alter this view. None of my friends knew any girls either (or if they did they never produced or spoke of them) which seems even stranger.

51

Perhaps strangest of all was that no girls so to speak appeared on the threshold of my life as a natural part of growing up, like beer and cigarettes, as novels say they do. Surely life should not have been discouraged simply because I did not dance and had no love of parties (I once retired to bed in the middle of the celebration of my own birthday)? How I reconciled this with my total acceptance of Lawrence I have no idea.

The first writing of mine ever to be printed appeared in the school magazine when I was twelve. It was a short facetious paragraph or two, reminding me that all my early contributions were in the manner of 'The Humourist', and all excruciating. I don't know why I can't be funny on paper—but it has been proved too often to need further demonstration. I can only say that when friends of mine had promoted to their own pages things I have said or written to them privately I have not felt that my jokes sounded unworthy of their reputations.

I never knew anyone in Coventry who was interested in writing. There may have been little groups who met and discussed each other's work, but I never came across them; nor was there at school any literary society where talent might try itself out. No pipe-lighting dominie (I am afraid I am falling into the style of my poem) casually slipped a well-worn volume into my hands as I was leaving his book-lined den ('by the way, you might care to have a look at this'): I did not much like the senior English master, and I do not think he much liked me. Of course none of this mattered. Thanks to my father, our house contained not only the principle works of most main English writers in some form or other (admittedly there were exceptions, like Dickens), but also nearly-complete collections of authors my father favoured— Hardy, Bennett, Wilde, Butler and Shaw, and later on Lawrence, Huxley and Katherine Mansfield. Not till I was much older did I realise that most boys of my class were brought up to regard Galsworthy and Chesterton as the apex of modern literature, and to think Somerset Maugham 'a bit hot'. I was therefore lucky. Knowing what its effect would be on me, my father concealed the existence of the Central Public Library as long as he could, but in the end the secret broke and nearly every evening I set off down Friar's Road with books to exchange. Many were returned unfinished, chosen because I had liked the thought of myself reading them. But for quite long periods I suppose I must have read a book a day, even despite the tiresome interruptions of morning and afternoon school.

Reading is not writing, though, and by then my ambition had pretty well deserted jazz drumming to settle upon a literary career. Apart from the school magazine I had still not got into print. I wrote ceaselessly, however; now verse, which I sewed up into little books, now prose, a thousand words a night after homework, resting my foolscap on Beethoven's Op. 132, the only classical album I possessed. Both were valueless, but I wish I could command that fluent industry today.

When the war broke out, I decided to go up to Oxford a year earlier than I had intended, since despite the Government's assurance that the 18 and 19 age groups would be registered last of all, no one knew when this would be once the fighting started in earnest. I felt it was imperative to have made some mark on the world before I did so, and during the cloudless summer of 1940 I sent four poems to *The Listener*. I was astonished when someone signing himself J.R.A. wrote back, saying that he would like to take one (it was the one I had put in to make the others seem better, but never mind). As I had hoped, it had not appeared before I nervously left for Oxford (changing trains, and stations, at Leamington), delaying until the issue of 28th October, just when I was ready for an injection of self-esteem. I remember buying several copies at Smith's in Cornmarket Street, and making sure that it was actually in each copy. Within a fortnight Coventry had been ruined by the German Air Force, and I never went back there to live again.

(First published in *Umbrella*, Vol 1, No. 3, Summer 1959.)

"The form the article was intended to take was that of a topic-by-topic gloss on 'I Remember', but it doesn't come over like this and I'm afraid people may think it is a considered account of my childhood, which of course it isn't. No doubt it will be exhumed eventually, if people still care . . ."

(Philip Larkin, letter to Harry Chambers 3rd August 1972.)

I REMEMBER, I REMEMBER
Philip Larkin

Coming up England by a different line
For once, early in the cold new year,
We stopped, and, watching men with number-plates
Sprint down the platform to familiar gates,
'Why, Coventry!' I exclaimed. 'I was born here.'

I leant far out, and squinnied for a sign
That this was still the town that had been 'mine'
So long, but found I wasn't even clear
Which side was which. From where those cycle-crates
Were standing, had we annually departed

For all those family hols? . . . A whistle went:
Things moved. I sat back, staring at my boots.
'Was that,' my friend smiled, 'where you "have your roots"?'
No, only where my childhood was unspent,
I wanted to retort, just where I started:

By now I've got the whole place clearly charted.
Our garden, first: where I did not invent
Blinding theologies of flowers and fruits,
And wasn't spoken to by an old hat.
And here we have that splendid family

I never ran to when I got depressed,
The boys all biceps and the girls all chest,
Their comic Ford, their farm where I could be
'Really myself'. I'll show you, come to that,
The bracken where I never trembling sat,

Determined to go through with it; where she
Lay back, and 'all became a burning mist'.
And, in those offices, my doggerel
Was not set up in blunt ten-point, nor read
By a distinguished cousin of the mayor,

Who didn't call and tell my father *There*
Before us, had we the gift to see ahead—
'You look as if you wished the place in Hell,'
My friend said, 'judging from your face.' 'Oh well,
I suppose it's not the place's fault,' I said.

'Nothing, like something, happens anywhere.'

'THE WHITSUN WEDDINGS'

Philip Larkin

It would, perhaps, be fitting for me to return the heartening compliment paid by the Selectors to *The Whitsun Weddings* with a detailed annotation of its contents. Unfortunately, however, once I have said that the poems were written in or near Hull, Yorkshire, with a succession of Royal Sovereign 2B pencils during the years 1955 to 1963, there seems little to add. I think in every instance the effect I was trying to get is clear enough. If sometimes I have failed, no marginal annotation will help now. Henceforth the poems belong to their readers, who will in due course pass judgment by either forgetting or remembering them.

If something must be said, it should be about the poems one writes not necessarily being the poems one wants to write. Some years ago I came to the conclusion that to write a poem was to construct a verbal device that would preserve an experience indefinitely by reproducing it in whoever read the poem. As a working definition, this satisfied me sufficiently to enable individual poems to be written. Insofar as it suggested that all one had to do was pick an experience and preserve it, however, it was much over-simplified. Nowadays nobody believes in 'poetic' subjects, any more than they believe in poetic diction. The longer one goes on, though, the more one feels that some subjects *are* more poetic than others, if only that poems about them get written whereas poems about other subjects don't. At first one tries to write poems about everything. Later on, one learns to distinguish somewhat, though one can still make enormously time-wasting mistakes. The fact is that my working definition defines very little: it makes no reference to this necessary element of distinction, and it leaves the precise nature of the verbal pickling unexplained.

This means that most of the time one is engaged in doing, or trying to do, something of which the value is doubtful and the mode of operation unclear. Can one feel entirely happy about this? The days when one could claim to be the priest of a mystery are gone: today mystery means either ignorance or hokum, neither fashionable qualities. Yet writing a poem is still not an act of the will. The distinction between subjects is not an act of the will. Whatever makes a poem successful is not an act of the will. In consequence, the poems that actually get written may seem trivial or unedifying, compared with those that don't. But the poems that get written, even if they do not please the will, evidently please that mysterious something that has to be pleased.

This is not to say that one is forever writing poems of which the will disapproves. What it does mean, however, is that there must be among the ingredients that go towards the writing of a poem a streak of curious self-gratification, almost impossible to describe except in some such terms, the presence of which tends to nullify any satisfaction the will might be feeling at a finished job. Without this element of self-interest, the theme, however worthy, can drift away and be forgotten. The situation is full of ambiguities. To write a poem is a pleasure: sometimes I deliberately let it compete in the open market, so to speak, with other spare-time activities, ostensibly on the grounds that if a poem isn't more entertaining to write than listening to records or going out it won't be entertaining to read. Yet doesn't this perhaps conceal a subconscious objection to writing? After all, how many of our pleasures really bear thinking about? Or is it just concealed laziness?

Whether one worries about this depends, really, on whether one is more interested in writing or in finding how poems are written. If the former, then such considerations become just another technical difficulty, like noisy neighbours or one's own character, parallel to a clergyman's doubts: one has to go on in spite of them. I suppose in raising them one is seeking some justification in the finished product for the sacrifices made on its behalf. Since it is the will that is the seeker, satisfaction is unlikely to be forthcoming. The only consolation in the whole business, as in just about every other, is that in all probability there was really no choice.

(First published in Poetry Book Society Bulletin No. 40, February 1964. *The Whitsun Weddings* was the Poetry Book Society Spring choice for 1964.)

PHILIP LARKIN ON POETRY

". . . one writes really to reproduce in other people the particular sensations or thoughts or emotions that you've had yourself. I don't know why one should do this, but that is the point of it—to construct a verbal device rather like a verbal penny-in-the-slot machine whereby, when the reader puts the penny of his attention into the machine, he gets the full sensation or emotion that provokes you to write the poem in the first place. One hopes this will go on happening long after one is dead and long after the Earth is inhabited by men from Mars and so on . . ."

(extract from *The Beverlonian* [Beverley Grammar School] interview, Vol. 19 No. 75, February 1976.)

". . . what I want readers to carry away from the poem in their minds is not the poem, but the experience; I want them to live something through the poem, without necessarily being conscious of the poem as a poem."

(extract from 'Speaking of Writing—XIII', *The Times*, February 20th 1974.)

"Poetry is memorable speech. I write when I feel strongly, and want to tell people . . . I have no enthusiasm for obscurity. Except, of course, for luminous and wonder-generating obscurity."

(extract from 'Two poets promenading', *Radio Times*, August 16th 1973.)

"I can think of one or two poets who are very clever intellectually, and who are trying to integrate all sorts of influences, but they don't make it emotionally. And poetry is a matter of emotion. . . . There is a sentence or two of Leslie Stephen, which Hardy used to be fond of, I can't remember it exactly, but it's something like 'The poet's task is to move our feelings by showing his own, and not to display his learning, or mimic the fine notes of his predecessors . . .' I've always thought it is a magnificent motto, for me anyway, it is the kind of thing I should like to think I did."

(extract from 'A conversation with Philip Larkin', *Tracks* No. 1, Summer 1967.)

"What I should like to do is write different kinds of poem that might be by different people. Someone said once that the great thing is not to be different from other people, but to be different from yourself."

(extract from 'Not Like Larkin', *The Listener*, 'Out of The Air', August 17th 1972.)

The visit of the American poet, Robert Lowell (extreme right), to the Brynmor Jones Library, 1 February 1973

POINT OF NO RETURN

Philip Larkin

THE OXFORD BOOK OF DEATH
Chosen and edited by D. J. Enright, *(Oxford, £9.50)*

Man's most remarkable talent is for ignoring death. For once the certainty of permanent extinction is realised, only a more immediate calamity can dislodge it from the mind, and then only temporarily. Yet on all sides people are booking foreign holidays, applying for permission to build sun-parlours, joining the Social Democratic Party. Truly, as Anatole France said, ignorance—in the sense of ignoring—is the necessary condition of life itself.

All the same, coming to terms with death has taken up a good deal of our time. Primarily in the form of religion: for if what distinguishes religion from ethics is the miraculous, the only miracle worth talking about is immortality. But there is also literature, where death is still the only possible end to a story, except marriage. Unfortunately, nothing is quite real in literature, not even death; either we are left feeling that in some indefinable way it is *all right*, or that the characters will get up unharmed and advance bowing to the footlights. This is not how death affects us in reality.

In this most audacious of Oxford anthologies, Dr Enright surveys what has been said on this colossal subject . . .

There is nothing didactic in Enright's approach: he does not tell us what to think or feel. Nevertheless, several recognisable attitudes emerge from his chorus of voices. First, of course, death isn't going to happen ('One short sleep past, we wake eternally'). Or, if it does happen, it is by definition something we needn't worry about ('so long as we exist, death is not with us; but when death comes, then we do not exist'). Or, if it does happen, it is jolly nice and comfortable ('in a sleep deeper and calmer than that of infancy, wrapped in the finest and softest dust'). Or, finally life would be very dull without death ('it is immeasurably heightened'), to me a view that fails to grip even more conspicuously than the others. It was thoroughly torpedoed by Kingsley Amis in 'Lovely' ('Look thy last on all things lovely/Every hour, an old shag said'), a poem I am sorry not to see included.

What might with some justice be called the majority view, however—death is the end of everything, and thinking about it gives us a pain in the bowels—is poorly represented. This is no doubt due to Dr Enright's tact as an anthologist. Unlike the Fat Boy, he doesn't want to make our flesh creep; slide after slide is whisked deftly away, with no chance to make a lasting impression. Nervous people need not be afraid of his pages. All the same, it may be wondered who will buy them. The volume hardly qualifies for the guest room, much less as a birthday or Christmas present. Whoever dreamed it up ('The Oxford Book of *Death!* How *marvellous!*') may have commercially miscalculated.

If so, serve them right. For in the last analysis the intrusion of death into our lives is so ruthless, so irreversible, so rarely unaccompanied by pain, terror and remorse, that to 'anthologise' it, however calmly, quizzically and compassionately, seems at best irrelevant, at worst an error of taste. 'Death and the sun are not to be looked at steadily,' says La Rochefoucauld, and by their nature anthologies do not look steadily, nor do they explain or console: they entertain. And death is not entertaining. The chapter on 'Care of the Dying' in any nursing manual makes this point more clearly.

(This is an extract from a review that was first published in *The Observer*, 24th April 1983.)

At his office desk, 5 April 1984

AUBADE

Philip Larkin

I work all day, and get half drunk at night.
Waking at four to soundless dark, I stare.
In time the curtain-edges will grow light.
Till then I see what's really always there:
Unresting death, a whole day nearer now,
Making all thought impossible but how
And where and when I shall myself die.
Arid interrogation: yet the dread
Of dying, and being dead,
Flashes afresh to hold and horrify.

The mind blanks at the glare. Not in remorse
—The good not done, the love not given, time
Torn off unused—nor wretchedly because
An only life can take so long to climb
Clear of its wrong beginnings, and may never;
But at the total emptiness for ever,
The sure extinction that we travel to
And shall be lost in always. Not to be here,
Not to be anywhere,
And soon; nothing more terrible, nothing more true.

This is a special way of being afraid
No trick dispels. Religion used to try,
That vast moth-eaten musical brocade
Created to pretend we never die,
And specious stuff that says *No rational being*
Can fear a thing it will not feel, not seeing
That this is what we fear—no sight, no sound,
No touch or taste or smell, nothing to think with,
Nothing to love or link with,
The anaesthetic from which none come round.

And so it stays just on the edge of vision,
A small unfocused blur, a standing chill
That slows each impulse down to indecision.

Most things may never happen: this one will,
And realisation of it rages out
In furnace-fear when we are caught without
People or drink. Courage is no good:
It means not scaring others. Being brave
Lets no one off the grave.
Death is no different whined at than withstood.

Slowly light strengthens, and the room takes shape.
It stands plain as a wardrobe, what we know,
Have always known, know that we can't escape,
Yet can't accept. One side will have to go,
Meanwhile telephones crouch, getting ready to ring
In locked-up offices, and all the uncaring
Intricate rented world begins to rouse.
The sky is white as clay, with no sun.
Work has to be done.
Postmen like doctors go from house to house.

(First published in T.L.S., 23rd December 1977.)

The visit of the poet Ted Hughes to Hull University, 30 May 1975.

NOTES ON CONTRIBUTORS

Harry Chambers, the publisher of *Peterloo Poets*, edited the special Larkin issue of *Phoenix* (Autumn/Winter 1973/74) and contributed a chapter to *Larkin at Sixty*, edited by Anthony Thwaite (*Faber and Faber Ltd.*, 1982.)

Robert Hull has recently published a book about language in schools. Another, on children's poetry is due in 1987.

Peter Levi is Professor of Poetry at Oxford. His *Selected Poems* are published by *Anvil Press*.

R. A. Maitre's first full collection, *Blue Barometers*, was published by *Peterloo Poets* in Autumn 1986.

Andrew Motion is the author of *Philip Larkin* in the 'Contemporary Writers' series (*Methuen*, 1982). He is writing the official *Biography* of Philip Larkin. A selection of his poems, *Dangerous Play: Poems 1974–1984*, has been published in the *King Penguin* series.

Meg Peacocke was a prizewinner in the 1986 Lancaster Festival of Literature poetry competition. Her first full collection, *Marginal Land*, will be published by *Peterloo Poets* in Spring 1988.

Craig Raine is poetry editor at *Faber and Faber Ltd.* His volumes of poetry include *Rich* (*Faber and Faber Ltd.*, 1984), *A Martian Sends A Postcard Home* (*OUP*, 1979) and *The Onion, Memory* (*OUP*, 1978).

William Scammell's third collection, *Jouissance* (*Peterloo Poets*, 1984), was a Poetry Book Society Recommendation. A fourth *Peterloo* collection will be published in 1987.

Vernon Scannell's *Selected Poems* are published by *Robson Books*. He received the Cholmondeley Award for Poetry (1974) and is one of the four judges of the 1986/87 *Peterloo Poets* Open Poetry Competition.

David Selzer is the author of *Elsewhere* (*E. J. Morten*, 1973). One of his poems was shortlisted in the 1986 TLS/Cheltenham Festival of Literature Poetry Competition.

David Sutton's third volume, *Flints*, was published by *Peterloo Poets*, Autumn 1986.

Anthony Thwaite is editing Larkin's *Collected Poems* and Larkin's *Selected Letters*. From 1973 to 1985 he was co-editor of *Encounter*. He was the editor of *Larkin at Sixty* (*Faber and Faber Ltd.*, 1982), reviews novels for *The Observer*, and is the Chairman of the 1986 Booker Award panel of judges. His volumes of poetry include *The Stones of Emptiness* (1967), *A Portion for Foxes* (1977) and *Victorian Voices* (1980).

PHOENIX ¹¹⁄₁₂

PHILIP LARKIN

a new poem
'Money'

and

worksheets of
'At Grass'

plus

critical articles

PHILIP LARKIN ISSUE

PETERLOO POETS